WORDS THEIR WAY

WORD STUDY IN ACTION • BIG BOOK OF RHYMES • WITHIN WORD PATTERN

Glenview, Illinois

Boston, Massachusetts

Chandler, Arizona

Upper Saddle River, New Jersey

PEARSON

ALWAYS LEARNING

D1637319

Contents

Twin Mix-Up

Jan and Jane look the same.

No one says the right name.

Jane complains to her twin, Jan.

"What a shame. We need a plan.

I'll wear one braid; you wear two.

Then I won't look the same as you."

Things to Do

What will I do today?

Let me think.

I'll swim in the sea

Or skate on the rink.

I'll ride my bike with a pal

Or climb a tree.

Who will have fun?

Kids like you and me.

Where Is That Clock?

Tick, tock, tick, tock.

Where are you, silly clock?

You woke me up but will not stop.

Are you by the phone or on the top?

Silly clock, where are you?

Oh, there you are—in my shoe!

I Like Bugs!

I think I like bugs.

I think this is true.

They're cute little things—

My favorites are blue.

But what I don't like

Is the way that they fly—

Up, down, and around,

Then right in my eye!

Jean's Dream

Jean had had ten red beads.

She kept them near her bed.

When she went to sleep one night,

Ideas popped in her head.

"I'll make a special necklace,

The best you've ever seen."

When Jean woke up that morning,

It was all just a dream.

My Summer Vacation

In June we camped in the van.

It was fun to make dinner in a pan.

In July I rode a train to my aunt.

I grew my own tomato plant.

In August I did a hike with my dad.

Summer is over, and I am sad.

Pancakes for Breakfast

When mom makes pancakes in a pan,

I eat as many as I can.

Two, four, six, eight—I can't wait

For stacks of pancakes on my plate.

"You ate them all," said my dad.

Mom will make more. I am glad!

The Cat Chaser

I have a dog named Ray

Who's as fast as he he can be.

He chases Nate the cat

Way up the big birch tree.

Nate feels right at home.

In his treetop space.

So Ray sits and waits for

Another cat to chase.

Let's Go to Grandma's!

We're off to see Grandma.

We hope she's's at home.

We'll take her some soap,

A mirror, and comb.

We'll follow the road.

We'll walk the whole way.

Now we're at Grandma's

We'll have a great day!

Follow the Wind

Where does the wind blow?

Through the trees, let's go!

Over the mountain covered in snow,

Wind blows everywhere we go.

By the seaside, over ocean foam,

Wind blows everywhere we roam.

The Snow Ride

"It's a fun ride in the snow!"

That's what I was told.

They roll across the hills,

Even though it's cold.

They take the road around the pond

And count the stars they find.

Most people come home chilly,

But they don't seem to mind.

Goodbye, Flu!

June is in her room with the flu.

She's such a sorry sight.

She'd like to get up from her bed.

She tries with all her might.

Mom brings a batch of fruit juice

And a very yummy lunch.

Soon June feels much better.

"Hey, Mom, thanks a bunch!"

Big Baby Sue

Baby Sue is huge.

We knew this from the start.

She grew so much so fast.

She needs a special cart.

We know that Sue is hard to budge.

You can judge yourself, it's true.

Now Sue's bigger than we are.

We're not sure what to do.

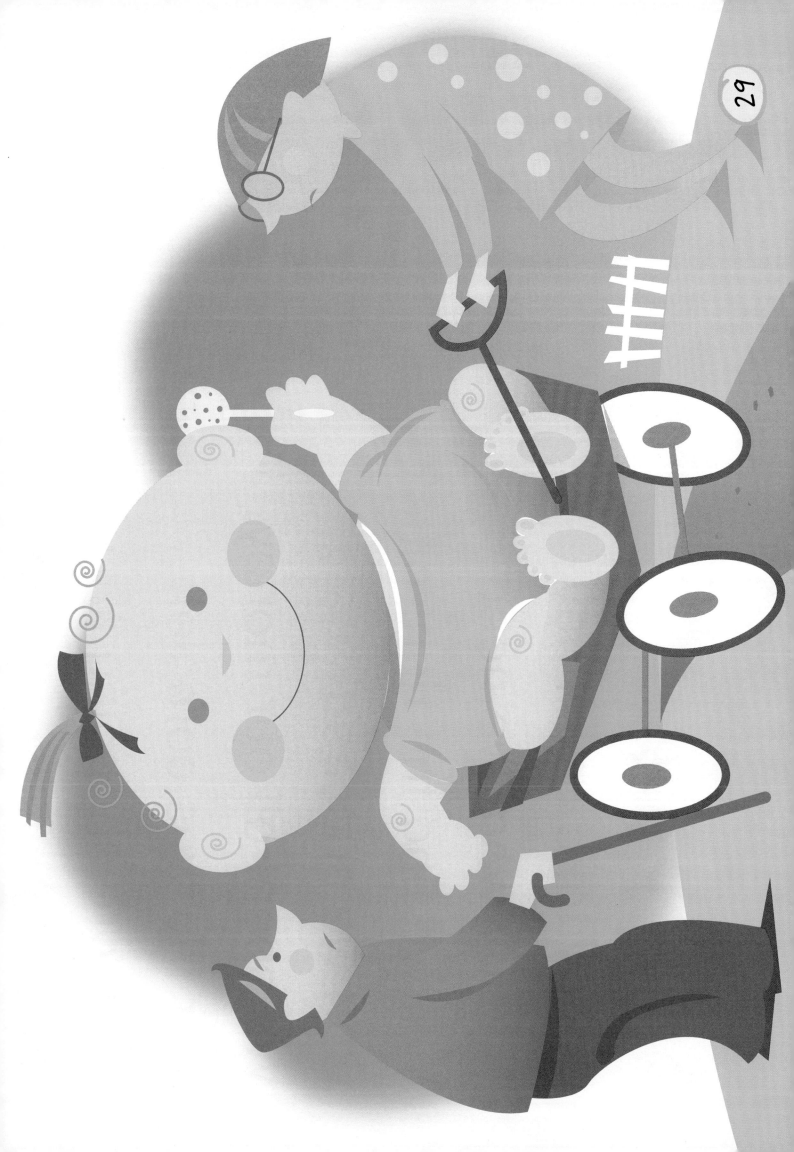

Shopping

It may take us all day

To buy what we need.

Will we find the right gifts?

Can we succeed?

We spent all our money.

Our trip was complete.

No more shopping for us.

We're totally beat!

Eagles Fly

Tilt your head up toward the sky.

See the eagle when it goes by?

How fun it must be

Gliding on a breeze.

Eagles fly through the air

And land in the trees.

A Bad Day

I hurt my head.

I tripped over my feet.

My sandwich fell out.

"Now what will I eat?"

I screamed and and I groaned

On this very bad day.

Then Mom gave me a hug,

And the pain went away.

Don't Cry

Hush, little brother, don't you cry.

Look at my kite flying high in the sky.

Up it goes for at least a mile.

It will be up there for a while.

Take the string and hold it in place.

Now a smile lights up your face.

Once Upon a Time

I chose a nice story,

To read to you today.

It starts with "Once upon a time,

In a land far, far away."

One day a kind prince went walking

By a wild dragon in a cave.

" I'll fight the dragon," said the prince,

" For I am very brave."

Third Base

As Barb played her favorite sport

She looked right at the umpire.

She guarded third base proudly

As the game came down to the wire.

She jumped so high to catch a ball,

She couldn't go much higher.

Fans around her burst into cheers,

"That girl's an awesome flier!"

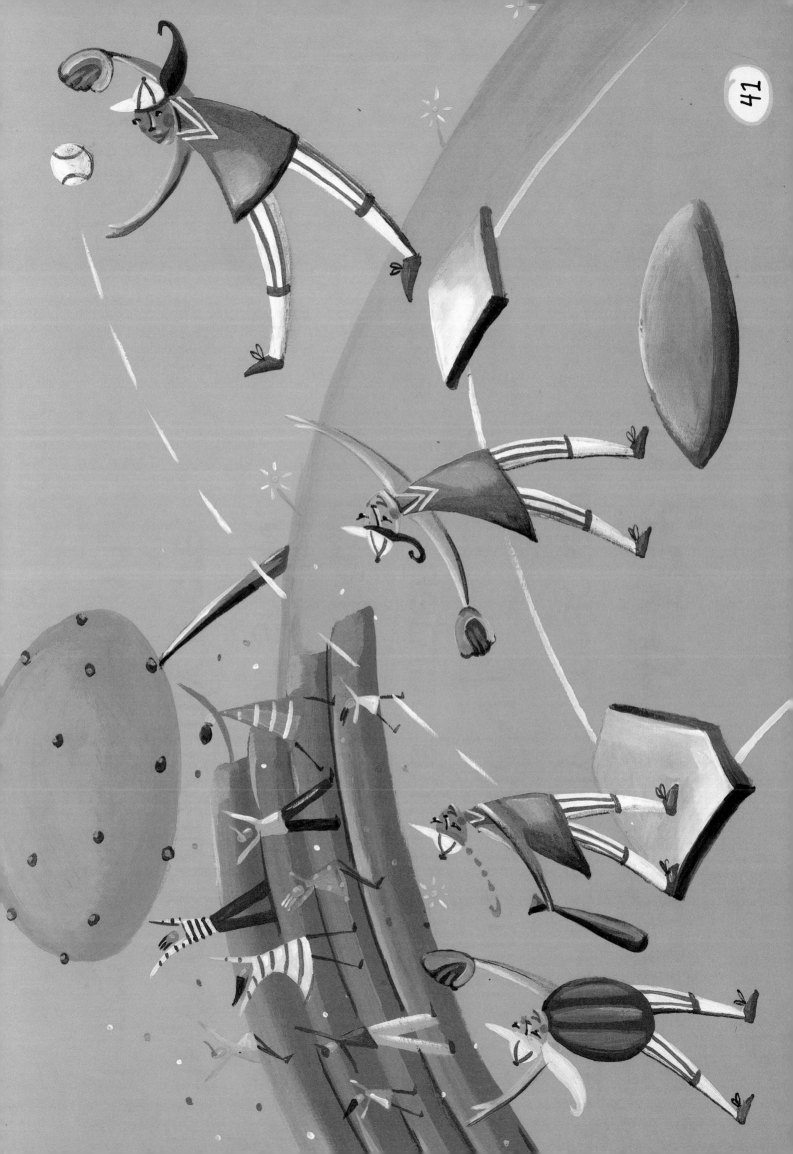

Scarecrow in the Garden

There is a silly scarecrow

Swaying in the air.

It stands in the garden

With a funny hat and hair.

Its arms are full of straw.

Its eyes, they only stare.

It may not be too smart,

But it gives the crows a scare.

Arctic Fox

Stay clear! There's Arctic Fox.

To you, he may seem small.

From his perch near his den,

He gives an eerie call.

In summer, Fox's fur is brown.

But watch it change in fall.

It ought to turn wintry white,

Then Fox can't be seen at all.

The Snoring Horse

Lion and Horse live next door.

Horse's loud snoring makes Lion roar,

"I can't take it anymore!"

So Lion buys earplugs

At the general store.

Now he can sleep.

They are friends forever more.

Watching for Sea Turtles

Sea turtles, sea turtles,

Where can they be?

With curved flippers, lay their eggs,

Then hurry out to sea.

They are magnificent!

Surely you agree?

Fern's Monsters

Monsters in the orchard!

Monsters in the park!

Fern doesn't like monsters—

Especially in the dark!

Monsters under her bed!

Large monsters in the store!

Just when Fern forgets them,

She bumps into some more!

Digging for Treasure

Treasure's hidden in the yard.

So we've been told!

Maybe we'll find some golden coins

Or something very very old.

Dig in the soil. Dig down deep.

I hope we find treasure

To enjoy and keep.

The Puppet Show

I made my puppet out of wood,

Paper, crayons, and glue.

My puppet show was soon to start.

All my lines I knew.

By noon my show had started.

I did it by the book.

When the show was over,

A graceful bow I took.

New Jeans Now!

I've outgrown my jeans.

How can that be?

They're now up past my ankles.

And there's a hole in one knee.

Now we go out to the mall

To find jeans that fit me.

I'll take any color—

The first pair I see!

The Lobster Boat

Out go the lobster crew.

At dawn they leave the land.

They sail on the ocean.

They search in the sand.

At last their cage is full.

They haul it up to check.

Lobsters with awesome claws

Come spilling out on deck.

Jake Bakes

There once was a chick

Whose name was Jake.

He liked to snack,

So he baked a cake.

He ignored the recipe

In the book.

The cake was awful.

Jake's NOT a good cook!

My Puppy Gus

I have a puppy named Gus.

He likes to wriggle.

He chases flies and gnats.

He makes me giggle!

He gnaws on furniture.

He puts on a show.

Will he grow out of it?

We'll soon know.

Running Squirrels

Squirrels run here and there.

Squirrels run everywhere.

They run into shrubs.

They run through the trees.

Squirrels seem so happy

Doing what they please.

The Journey

It was the stroke of midnight,

On a strange and musty ship.

The nights were dark and cold

On our long, rough ocean trip.

There were only scraps for meals.

The ocean spray was wet.

We've come so far to find a home.

We know we'll get there yet!

Goose Goes to the City

Goose lived in the country.

Giraffe lived at the zoo.

Goose went for a visit.

Right to the city she flew.

Cars zoomed all around.

The noise was too much!

Goose flew back home.

Giraffe said, " Keep in touch!"

ISBN-13: 978-1-4284-3243-7
ISBN-10:   1-4284-3243-4
12 13 14 15 16 V064 18 17 16 15